This journal belongs to:

....

Date ....

I found it is the small everyday deeds of ordinary folk that keep the darkness at bay...small acts of kindness and love.

J. R. R. TOLKIEN

*Y*ou are a beloved child of God, precious to Him
in every way. As you seek Him, He will show you
the mysteries of life and unfold His unique plans for you—
a life full of rich blessing and compassionate kindness.

God cares about you and knows all the desires of your
heart. He is as close as breathing. Let this journal inspire
you to express your thoughts, record your prayers,
embrace your dreams, and always be kind.

*D*o all the good you can, by all the means you can,
in all the ways you can, in all the places you can, at all the times you can,
to all the people you can, as long as ever you can.

JOHN WESLEY

*T*hose who bring sunshine into the lives of others cannot keep it from themselves.

JAMES M. BARRIE

Kind words can be short and easy to speak,
but their echoes are truly endless.
MOTHER TERESA

*D*on't think too much about yourself.
Try to cultivate the habit of thinking of others; this will reward you.

CHARLES W. ELIOT

....

....

....

....

....

....

....

....

....

....

....

....

....

....

....

....

....

....

....

....

....

....

....

Anxiety weighs down the heart, but a kind word cheers it up.

THE BIBLE

....
....
....
....
....
....
....
....
....
....
....
....
....
....
....
....
....
....
....
....
....
....
....
....

I expect to pass through life but once. If, therefore,
there be any kindness I can show, or any good thing I can do to any fellow being,
let me do it now, and not defer or neglect it, as I shall not pass this way again.

WILLIAM PENN

*S*ince you get more joy out of giving to others,
you should put a good deal of thought into the happiness that you are able to give.

ELEANOR ROOSEVELT

A tree is known by its fruit; a man by his deeds. A good deed is never lost;
he who sows courtesy reaps friendship, and he who plants kindness gathers love.

SAINT BASIL

*Be kind to one another, tenderhearted,
forgiving one another, as God in Christ forgave you.*

THE BIBLE

No act of kindness, no matter how small, is ever wasted.

AESOP

*K*indness is like snow; it beautifies everything it covers.

ANONYMOUS

*T*he first question which the priest and the Levite asked was: "If I stop to help this man, what will happen to me?" But...the Good Samaritan reversed the question: "If I do not stop to help this man, what will happen to him?"

MARTIN LUTHER KING JR.

*T*hink of ways to motivate one another to acts of love and good works.

THE BIBLE

*K*ind deeds often come back to the givers in fairer shapes than they go.
LOUISA MAY ALCOTT

If we all do just one act of kindness daily,
we just might set the world in the right direction.

MARTIN KORNFELD

*A*s much as we need a prosperous economy,
we also need a prosperity of kindness and decency.

CAROLINE KENNEDY

*Carry out a random act of kindness, with no expectation of reward,
safe in the knowledge that one day someone might do the same for you.*

DIANA, PRINCESS OF WALES

Do not let kindness and truth leave you; bind them around your neck, write them on the tablet of your heart.

THE BIBLE

What does love look like? It has the hands to help others.
It has the feet to hasten to the poor and needy. It has the eyes to see misery and want.
It has the ears to hear the sighs and sorrows of men. That is what love looks like.

SAINT AUGUSTINE

A little consideration, a little thought for others, makes all the difference.

A. A. MILNE

I am only one, but I am still one. I cannot do everything,
but still I can do something. And because I cannot do everything,
I will not refuse to do the something that I can do.

HELEN KELLER

*K*indness is a hard thing to give away. It keeps coming back to the giver.
RALPH SCOTT

Be devoted to one another in love. Honor one another above yourselves.

THE BIBLE

_____

_____

_____

_____

_____

_____

_____

_____

_____

_____

_____

_____

_____

_____

_____

_____

_____

_____

_____

_____

_____

_____

_____

_____

*L*et us learn to live with kindness, to love everyone, even when they do not love us.
POPE FRANCIS

*A*sk yourself: Have you been kind today? Make kindness
your modus operandi [your way of operating] and change your world.

ANNIE LENNOX

Kind words are the music of the world.
FREDERICK WILLIAM FABER

*T*hree things in human life are important: The first is to be kind; the second is to be kind; and the third is to be kind.

HENRY JAMES

Command them to do good, to be rich in good deeds,
and to be generous and willing to share.

THE BIBLE

*K*indness is the evidence of greatness.

CHARLES FENNO HOFFMAN

*F*or beautiful eyes, look for the good in others; for beautiful lips, speak only words of kindness; and for poise, walk with the knowledge that you are never alone.

AUDREY HEPBURN

The greatest thing a man can do for his heavenly Father
is to be kind to some of His other children.

HENRY DRUMMOND

Kindness does not require us to be blind to facts or to live in fancies, but it does require us to cherish a habit of goodwill, ready to show pity if sorrow appears, and slow to turn away even if hostility appears.

ALEXANDER MACLAREN

No one has ever seen God; but if we love one another,
God lives in us and his love is made complete in us.

THE BIBLE

You never lose by loving. You only lose by holding back.

BARBARA DE ANGELIS

No man can do me a truer kindness in this world than to pray for me.

CHARLES SPURGEON

....
....
....
....
....
....
....
....
....
....
....
....
....
....
....
....
....
....
....
....
....
....
....
....
....
....

If I can put one touch of rosy sunset into the life of any man or woman,
I shall feel that I have worked with God.

GEORGE MACDONALD

Kindness is in our power, even when fondness is not.

SAMUEL JOHNSON

Let there be kindness in your face, in your eyes, in your smile, in the warmth of your greeting.... Don't only give your care, but give your heart as well.

MOTHER TERESA

*G*reat is his steadfast love toward us; and the faithfulness of the LORD endures for ever.

THE BIBLE

All doors open to courtesy.

THOMAS FULLER

*K*ind words do not cost much. Yet they accomplish much.

BLAISE PASCAL

*T*here is a grace of kind listening, as well as a grace of kind speaking.

FREDERICK WILLIAM FABER

*T*he really great man is the man who makes every man feel great.

G. K. CHESTERTON

*Your own soul is nourished when you are kind;
it is destroyed when you are cruel.*
THE BIBLE

When we are inclined towards someone, we can hardly preserve our heart in quietness; usually we will be stirred by our emotion to seek feverishly to please the other one.

WATCHMAN NEE

*L*ife is an exciting business, and most exciting when it is lived for others.
HELEN KELLER

The whole idea of compassion is based on a keen awareness
of the interdependence of all these living beings,
which are all part of one another, and all involved in one another.

THOMAS MERTON

*T*rue benevolence, or compassion, extends itself through the whole of existence and sympathizes with the distress of every creature capable of sensation.

JOSEPH ADDISON

Do to others as you would like them to do to you.

THE BIBLE

Compassion takes imagination.

JENNIFER BEALS

*R*emember that everyone you meet is afraid of something,
loves something, and has lost something.

I choose kindness. I will be kind to the poor, for they are alone. Kind to the rich, for they are afraid. And kind to the unkind, for such is how God has treated me.

MAX LUCADO

*D*on't forget to show hospitality to strangers, for some who have done this
have entertained angels without realizing it!

THE BIBLE

We must never minimize the suffering of another. Scripture's mandate to us is,
Weep with them that weep (Romans 12:15).

BILLY GRAHAM

*P*eople may excite in themselves a glow of compassion,
not by toasting their feet at the fire, and saying: Lord, teach me compassion,
but by going and seeking an object that requires compassion.

HENRY WARD BEECHER

What comes from the heart goes to the heart.

SAMUEL TAYLOR COLERIDGE

....

....

....

....

....

....

....

....

....

....

....

....

....

....

....

....

....

....

....

....

....

....

....

....

How far you go in life depends on your being tender with the young, compassionate with the aged, sympathetic with the striving, and tolerant of the weak and strong. Because some day in life you will have been all of these.

GEORGE WASHINGTON CARVER

*G*od is not unjust; he will not forget your work and the love you have shown him
as you have helped his people and continue to help them.

THE BIBLE

By compassion we make others' misery our own,
and so, by relieving them we relieve ourselves also.

As small as it may seem, a good deed is always worth the doing.

SPARK MATSUNAGA

How beautiful a day can be when kindness touches it!

GEORGE ELLISTON

*O*ne who knows how to show and to accept kindness
will be a friend better than any possession.

SOPHOCLES

*L*et us not grow weary while doing good,
for in due season we shall reap if we do not lose heart.

THE BIBLE

To keep the Golden Rule we must put ourselves in other people's places,
but to do that consists in and depends upon picturing ourselves in their places.

HARRY EMERSON FOSDICK

I have always held firmly to the thought that each one of us can do a little
to bring some portion of misery to an end.

ALBERT SCHWEITZER

A good character is the best tombstone. Those who loved you and were helped by you will remember you when forget-me-nots have withered. Carve your name on hearts, not on marble.

CHARLES H. SPURGEON

Be merciful, just as your Father is merciful.

THE BIBLE

*U*nless someone like you cares a whole awful lot,
nothing is going to get better. It's not.

<small>DR. SEUSS</small>

*T*he act of giving and receiving is where the real magic of human connection occurs.
LEON LOGOTHESIS

We love because [God] first loved us.

THE BIBLE

*L*ove and kindness are never wasted. They always make a difference. They bless the one who receives them, and they bless you, the giver.

BARBARA DE ANGELIS

It is in giving that we receive.

SAINT FRANCIS OF ASSISI

A single act of kindness throws out roots in all directions,
and the roots spring up and make new trees.

AMELIA EARHART

*K*indness makes a person attractive. If you would win the world,
melt it, do not hammer it.

ALEXANDER MACLAREN

*L*et us make one point, that we meet each other with a smile, when it is difficult to smile. Smile at each other, make time for each other in your family.

MOTHER TERESA

*A*fter you have been kind, after Love has stolen forth into the world and done
its beautiful work, go back into the shade again and say nothing about it.

HENRY DRUMMOND

*K*ind words produce their own image in men's souls; and a beautiful image it is.
They soothe and quiet and comfort the hearer. They shame him out of his sour,
morose, unkind feelings. We have not yet begun to use kind words
in such abundance as they ought to be used.

BLAISE PASCAL

*C*onstant kindness can accomplish much. As the sun makes ice melt,
kindness causes misunderstanding, mistrust, and hostility to evaporate.

ALBERT SCHWEITZER

Ellie Claire® Gift & Paper Expressions
Franklin, TN 37067
EllieClaire.com
Ellie Claire is a registered trademark of Worthy Media, Inc.

Always Be Kind Journal
© 2017 by Ellie Claire
Published by Ellie Claire, an imprint of Worthy Publishing Group, a division of Worthy Media, Inc.

ISBN: 978-1-63326-165-5

Stock or custom editions of Ellie Claire titles may be purchased in bulk for educational, business, ministry, fund-raising, or sales promotional use. For information, please e-mail info@EllieClaire.com.

Cover and interior art by shutterstock.com

Compiled by Jill Jones
Cover and interior design by Melissa Reagan

Printed in China

1 2 3 4 5 6 7 8 9 – RRD – 22 21 20 19 18 17